LOVE, LUST AND OTHER ENTANGLEMENTS

DAVID GLASMAN

Copyright © 2017 by David Glasman
All rights reserved. No part of this publication may be reproduced, distributed, or transmitted in any form or by any means, including photocopying, recording, or other electronic or mechanical methods, without the prior written permission of the publisher, except in the case of brief quotations embodied in critical reviews and certain other non-commercial uses permitted by copyright law.

INTRODUCTION

These poems are a hymn to our struggle to find belonging, love, family and home in our modern lives. How do we connect with others, the world, our wildness, our dreams and spectres? Most importantly, how do we connect with ourselves? Drawing on his experience of love and loss, and of joy and despair, David Glasman's poems are rich in observation and imagery, grounded in the body and the soil. At times reflective, at times urgent, always they are alive and seeking to find the answers. It is poetry of the gut, poetry of dark days and sunlit skies and all the shades of dappling inbetween.

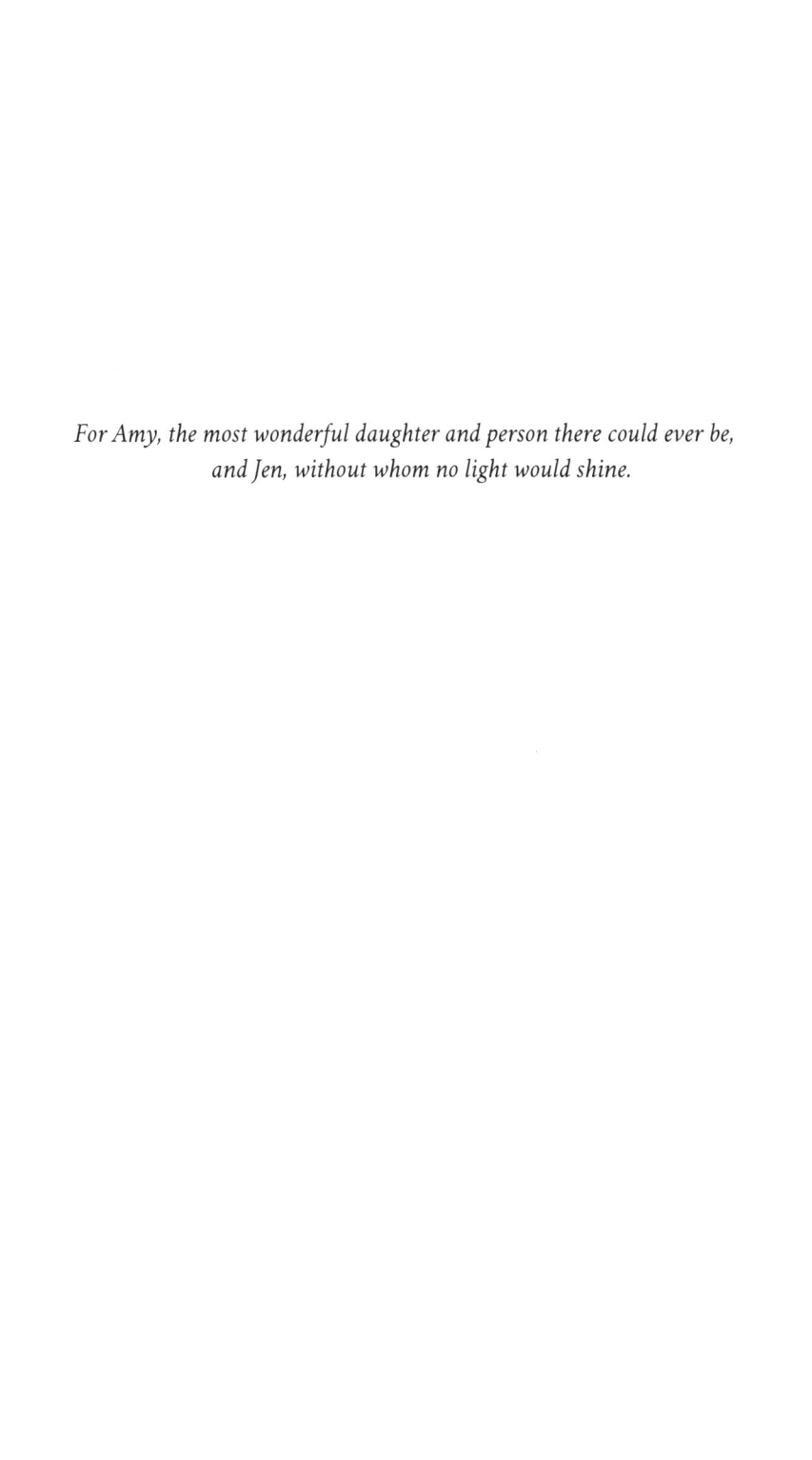

For Amy, the most wonderful daughter and person there could ever be, and Jen, without whom no light would shine.

AN ARDENT WISH

When will love make a home in my heart,
Get out the ladders and brushes and the decorating start,
Bring in the beds, put up some shelves,
With pots and pans kit out the kitchen
Where curries deepen and soups boil
While spice and welcome in the steamed air coil?
When will love billow fresh cotton sheets,
Entice from the yard hydrangeas and roses
Dig peas and spuds from the alkaline soil,
Hang postcards and photos on the walls,
And, from them all, memories and stories
Rich and tall?

When will love pull up the blinds,
Open the windows, let pleasure ring
In every squeaky tread
On every well-worn floorboard,
Let light reveal the thank you in every scattered shoe,
Each towel wet with showered singing?
When let fun adorn cooking and cleaning

And breathe lust and longing
Into every fibre of our bed?

For it can, if I would but let it.

Long ago, in another house, a child decided
It could not be so:
Giants ranged in the world,
Who were angry and invaded homes.
They trampled little boys if they made a noise
Or let known their need for kitchens and stairs.
And the world with its messages of competition and shame
Made it clear it was best
To build a structure of one's own
Where pretty objects gather and people come and go
And no-one stays long enough
To find you eat from tins
And don't wash your clothes.

When will love make a home in my heart?
Perhaps I am ready to start,
To hear each sunrise whispering:
"When you throw a door open each new day,
And no longer abide the pain of apart,
But let the pain of together
Begin."

LOVE, LUST AND OTHER ENTANGLEMENTS

A QUESTION

Shocked, I see you,
In my bathroom, naked.
No, I feel you, your fierce tenderness,
Your tender fierceness.
It's there as you lean toward the mirror,
Eyeliner in hand,
Your weight
Held in thigh, ham and hip,
Your joy bounded in lips that pucker and grip,
The curves of you,
The strength surging,
Elegantly,
From haunch to splayfoot fire red toes.
Cleopatra, Clytemnestra, Gaga and Garbo.
You are so clear in your trusting,
So alive in your thrusting.
I quake.
You are an urgent question
Standing on the cold ceramic of my prose:

"I'm real. Here. Home.
Are you?"

WALKING

The walk from Hammersmith Bridge to Barnes
Was a rather plain affair.
The pubs were shut,
It being Sunday and past two,
The Thames lazily low.

At first we were content to admire the charms
Of Palladian and Regency houses,
Looking not quite so grand
Under a greying sky
Streaked by planes bound (unromantically)
For the airport at Heathrow.

Halfway to Chiswick we linked arms,
Familiar in well-known surroundings
Of pavements stained by gum,
Lock-up garages,
Lace curtains that blurred the sport,
Here and there, a crow.

Before Barnes Bridge the North-Easterly calmed,
And a solitary rower,
Lifting oars with shoulders stroked by sun,
Created rings in the water,
That radiated silently, row by row.

Back again, across the river, we crossed palms,
But said no word about it.
Exchanging banter that swelled
From simple phrases
Until it seemed Thames' banks
Burst in blessed overflow.

On the walk from Hammersmith Bridge to Barnes,
We traced the river's course,
Tied shy love with Thames' ancient bow.

ROMANCE

I was going to write of finer feelings,
Love, bonds, beauty, romance -
All that jazz.

How her bracelets' colours -
The reds, blues, gold and greens -
Were like the patina of our affection,
Burning the sky in a Tuscan scene.

How the carnations in the vase -
Their buds, pink, delicate and pure -
Were as the simplicity of our love
With devotion and truth alone at its core.

How the bin, too, with its collection of paper
Told a story of sex
Uncomplicated and fun
Bodies coiling yet unknotting
Tight chests, arms, legs.

Of these things I was going to write,
And more – how pictures hung on walls,
Books lined on shelves, clothes packed,
Records stacked, told of two people
Making a stab at home because we are
Such in-love fools.

When in she bursts, drunk (on champagne!) still.
And the force of her tongue
Tears through all rhymes
And her breath, angry and searching,
Burns
For real.

YEARNING 1

She is the vessel of all my yearning
The black and the white of it,
The seething and the scythe,
The dark and the light of it,
The keening and the cry.

Visceral the churning.
It is the blood that lives
And the blood that dies,
It is the menstrual breach dripping down the thigh,
It is the unrelenting eye
Marching up the stocking seam,
The sweaty palm fevered now for flesh
In all its dangerous burning,
Trembling over hidden valleys and rising skirts,
Yearning, yearning for a diamond
In the ditch and the dirt,
Limbs of lava, leaking juice,
Squirming.

Desire.
My desire.
It is the ice in the fire,
Spring's unslated thirst drowning Winter
With braggard bulbs and ravenous shoots
Rampaging their way through earth,
A lust sated yesterday that today
Cannot be sated.
It is the bullet that cannot be stopped,
The train that cannot be halted,
The mare, thick of haunch and blank of eye,
That bellows as it is mated.
I am the High Priest in the temple
Hands hot above the disembowelled child,
Mothers pleading, ages of them, piled,
In hand a dripping knife,
A reminder of the crimson truth
In stench and entrails and bile,
The human is but an animal pretending not to be wild.

But over the red thrum I hear
A song of strange celebration:
Ancient hags incant above a primal brew
A charm of all that stinks in earth,
Bone, spittle, juice of me and you,
As we make love under a vaulting sky
As dark as any afterbirth.
And amidst the roar there rises
A discant dotted with joy.
The women gathering let loose a howl,
Scratch the air with shriek,
Hallelujah lust's blessing, its fecund messing,
The ecstasy of its dark Arctic heat.

HUG

You held me
And for a moment
Yielded that which you would not have me know -
That for many mornings
You too snuggled up to cold air
Huddled under linen sheets fresh and spare
Placed frozen toes
On calves that were your own,
Touched alone the tidy clothes,
The toaster,
The hardness of a chair.
Heard bare voices from the street.
Touching, you ignite
Under your breasts
Memories, harrowing.

But, briefly, in press and heat,
We felt a whole life's love,
Given and withheld.

Chasms of it,
Narrowing.

AFTERWARDS

Afterwards we dressed
Our hardwon intimacy expressed
In the casual observance of each other's body:
This mole on the right shoulder,
That roll of fat,
Those freckles dotting the back:
The vessel of our journeys seen
By another being.
We honoured the beautiful mundane
Of a bra clip fastened, a shirt buttoned,
Just that.

Afterwards we expressed
Our well guarded separateness
In backs turned away
From our bed's delicious union
To the calculation of the clock-ruled day:
We staked claim again to our body's
Stories and their boundaries,
Marked our territory with underwear and skirts,

With cotton shirts exchanged for cotton sheets,
And not so loving remarks,
While with sex-scented fingers we pulled
Synthetic socks onto our feet.

Afterwards we left
The place, that nest
Of entanglement where again and again
We hoped and dared to meet,
And carried the memory in our bodies
Of this thigh caressed, this nipple pressed,
Through our carwash worlds.
Soaped clean by meetings, sheened by joshings and jests,
We moved further apart -
Where we touched playfully toe to toe
Now shoe-shod,
The joyous chaos of our naked flesh,
Now emailed and filed, shut fast behind a desk.

And long afterwards,
After many afterwards,
Though the moments of afterwards are less,
The separation of work cannot erase
What our bodies remember
As if still together,
The heat of each other,
The tenderness of the other's caress.

LUST

The pigeon, lust, has a funny kind of freedom.
On streets stained with gum
He pecks for crumbs,
Casually dropped.
At the last minute he dodges cars,
But he doesn't fly far
For his wings are losing their feathers
And maybe there's spleen in the roadkill.
Loitering near the spikes of high-heel shoes
And Doc Marten boots,
He coos at the firmness of a lycra arse
Seen from below with a furtive glance.
Not bad. That'll do.
But I guess even a shabby bird dreams
Amidst the lurid stream of commerce, cash and craving,
That one day -
One dazzling, diaphonous day -
This life of circling on the sidelines,
Of fighting for scraps,
Of being the winged rat of street skulking survival,

He'll metamorphise in the potion pool of love
And become his envied cousin
A beautiful, pure white dove.

But what then for him, the lust?
What pavement would be without its pigeon?
Where stage shame's recurring dream
Of the tyrant boy and the tyrant father
Clashing in the cavernous footlights between;
What the place, where the day
For an unloved scavenger
Dragging its gangrene foot, preening its stunted wing,
What the home and where the street
For creature aglow with grime
And gloriously bright with sin?

SUSPENSION BRIDGE

A gull appeared silently above my head.
It cut the crisp winter morning with its wings
Curved and strong.
It eyes the river's slow mud for worms,
Gracefully readying its sharp feet and hooked beak.
Underneath both it and I
The Avon creeps as quietly by
Through the bridge-brinked gorge
To water the city.
I sit at the cliff's edge.
I know the gull, the river, the leaves
Breaking into fire before they fall,
Can speak with me. But I am deaf
To their simple call. I,
I am fear, fear instead,
Fear that I am not, nor ever will be.
It clutches the throat, squeezes my chest,
Chokes off the voice that would be heard.
Through the quietude a buzzard's cry
Is an alarm, desperate and absurd.

I choose, though, to feel the moment.
Without urgency I let the sun burn
One cheek, the cold scratch the other.
I am not going deep, though,
And reach across to you.
If Brunel can span the sky, why not I?
The miracle of telephony throws your voice into the clear blue air.
Contractions of breath and throat
Through many masks and one receiver
Coalesce miraculously here.
Something stirs. Love.
But we tried that once.
Still it seems we cannot quite let go,
Like this bridge of hammer and daring
That inhabits the air between two ancient banks.
It seems I met you somewhere precarious
Distracted by the promptings of vertigo.

Our talking ends and I sit on
On the bench.
The gull is long gone
But the river moves still
And the construction of chain and steel
Continues to be
A possibility of bridging,
Holding lovers suspended on ground above ground,
While the Avon flows between city and sea.

BLACK DOGS AND OTHER CAVERNOUS SPACES

DAFFODILS

You cannot hear daffodils grow
As they bloom from tight buds
Into the surprised air.
The petals break and part quietly,
Their trumpet mouths blare silently in the night.
Here, on an oval table in a square room,
They fan out in primal delight.

But what of me,
What of the humanity
That dwells in the glasses that lie on the desk beside?
I cannot feel my soul grow.
When daffodils bud they bloom and be.
But what of me?

In Yad Vashem there is a photograph
In faded black and white
Of ragged bodies piled high.
This is not man, thrusting, bursting, bright.
This is not bloom. It is blight.

I am appalled but do not cry.
Then, at the sight of hundreds of discarded spectacles,
My parched soul undams:
This, this is the man.

I see each one breaking bread,
Hear each haggling over price,
Feel them climb heavily into bed,
Worry over houses, dream of a devout wife,
Taste the sweat of baker, surgeon, miner, clerk,
Husband, father, son,
Someone loving and loved.
Someone.

Could this be my well, my baptismal birth?
Will then my blooming be
The silent flame of a rioting universe?

SITTING

Sitting still
I join the world of still things,
That mug, that chair,
These logs in the fireplace
Each day gathering dust
As I come and go on my busy way:
The portrait on the wall,
Photographs framing people and places
Visited and unvisited.
Still too, a spider plant,
A shelf of books.
Left to be, they rest peacefully.

My friends.
Gently taking my hand
You guide me to another stillness:
The humming silence.
Both in and out, she calls.
She always has and always will,
Knowing she is nothing to run in terror from,

An invitation to embrace not annihilate
With noise.

In.

I walk through a space more blood than ballast,
More womb than wall,
And there, somewhere near my heart, I guess,
Is a boy, arms outstretched.
He wants to be held.
He's been here alone a long time.
Something to do with mother's fingers being cold,
With anger living in sound
As the two child-adults shouted away their fears
And disappointments. Noise was never safe.
From here, I know too, the boy
Believes the world is but a place
Peopled by giants who roar
And tread his space with clumsy shoes.

I gather him in,
Feel his heart pound as he clings,
The passion of his grip.
Love was never his.
So I too hold,
Falling together into stillness,
Breath by breath,
Heartbeat by heartbeat.
In measure
We fall, together.

Welcome, my boy,
Keeper of terror and joy.
Once calm, we'll play.

But for now, rain is falling
And I feel the land
Coming to life
As it always knew it would
In sacred silent waters.

ABANDONED

Not to know love when one is young
Is to be abandoned
In a cathedral,
Consecrated and great,
And feel
An indifferent chill
In the ancient sacred space.

FEAR

Fear, the carrion crow,
Swept down to mock
The fledgling chicks of Hope
That nested in my heart.
It goaded their nascent bodies,
Thick still in ambiotic fluid,
Their blind eyes, their flightless wings,
Their beaks searching and open.
It was so close they smelt its snarl.
The fledglings shiver in the cold it brings.
For an eternal moment,
It seems to destroy the sun.
Before the crow returns to its tree
As if, in a universe of arching sky,
Burgeoning birth of green,
It is the feature that must be seen,
Waiting always for carrion.

WHEN

When I fret and gnaw
At the threads of despair
Conjure from the yet-formed air
The man ever orphaned
From intimacy's abundant fare
And silently howl, "Not for me
Her whisper in the ear
That turns sweat soaked sheets
Into the comfort of the sea,
No, not for me, not for me,
Her head pillowed on my chest
Its weight sinking into the peace
Of home's return, its place of rest."
Not for me, no, not for me,
The hand that spells I care
When a million thorns of indifference
Prick the delicate skin until raw and bare.
No, not for me,
The cradle of intimacy.
Then, then, I walk in outside's in,

Jolt with joy at cherry blossoming,
How sunlight plays, a chiffchaff sings,
A beech sways, a leaf greens, shimmering.
Then I hear the earth,
Her ancient calling,
A blessing that never stops falling:
"You are here, Your day is come,
Welcome as always, my son,
My son."

BEING SEPARATE

I sit and watch another's pain,
Watch him shout words to nobody I can see
Commune with those he still hopes
To reach, though they never loved him before
And do not now. He holds tight
That one day they might, they just might.
"Hey yeah, that would be cool,
D'you know what I mean, know what I mean."
His words tumble out wanting to be heard.
They drive his body to express
In this bourgeois place of roasted coffee, wifi and chat
That un-nice thing -
An honest dream shattered
And a person at war with himself.
Shards of people forever present, forever away,
Held at bay by a finger clicked, a foot
Tapped, and a phone
He hopes will ring one day.

I watch and long to rise,

To put an arm around him and say…
I don't know…maybe just,"It's Okay,
You're Okay."

But I don't.
I leave him in pain.
He rages on, clearly distressed.

Something about our current space
Compartmentalises our hearts.
We sip coffee, digest the news,
Hold tight to our own phones;
Are so scared to reach
Even to the lost in us
Scared to be rejected by our tenuous club,
That we are witnesses to and actors in
Scenes of separation,
Averting eyes from the one in the corner,
With-holding arms,
Defiantly separate
Each to each.

I rise instead and leave.
I do not know what happened to that man,
Whether he found a hand to hold
That was not cold and spectral.
But I know that that day
The news was hard to take
And my coffee a little bitter.

BOY

He's still here, the boy in the photograph,
Still backing away.
Still caging his beating heart,
Biting his lip, half smiling,
Looking at the world with a sidelong glance
As if to ask:
"This joy I feel, this power I have
To love, laugh, shout and play,
Is it Okay?
Am I Okay?"

He must be aged about two.
Four at most.
In his bones he already carries fear:
The hunched shoulders, the twisted neck,
The tightened jaw.
There's been so much shouting.
He is sure, though he knows not why,
They'll be so much more.

But there's love in his eyes too,
And the need for love.
From his perch on the upright piano
He speaks to the camera and says:
"If you promise to receive it,
As you sometimes do
With whispering like summer winds
And arms like summer skies,
Then take it, take it,
All of it, of me, for you."
On film, the little boy is caught
Hovering between the two.

He hovers still,
Dressed in the jumper his grandmother knitted
Stitch by stitch with gossip and care,
Sporting still a wobbly fringe and unruly hair.
His legs still dangle,
Podgy calves and podgy feet enclosed in bright red sandals.
But now, a tyrant boy, his twin,
Also still dwells within.
He is an unrelenting critic:
His parents' violence and distance fixed
In his contemptuous grin.
He bides no excuses for himself or the world,
We're useless and riddled with sin.

Sad how early the problems set in.

I yearn to set the little boy free,
But it's so long and so deep.
To have him look me straight in the eye,
His features, at last, full of ease,

To let him loose to play,
To meet him face to face,
Man and boy in pride and joy,
In daylight's present grace,
And his little fingers squeeze
In the tenderest embrace.

A HAND ON THE SHOULDER

I long to feel God's hand on my shoulder,
Comforting, gently pressed,
Whispering softly as Love's caress:
"You can stop trying now, your pain is over."

But I know it is not to be,
That He or She demands a greater test,
That it is I, I,
Who must somehow find his best
When everything and everyone has fled,
When bitterness fills my head,
When dreams of home have collapsed into a flat
That holds a despairing man
Lying in an empty bed, staring at an empty crack.

People say, "Each and everyday
Be kind, be patient."
Self-help guides extol the virtues
Of daily practice, of following a path,
Of keeping on:

"Create, and the seed will inevitably grow."
And I know, or want to know
That they are right,
That if I keep treading I will clear a way,
That if I can keep loving I will nurture a new light.

So, that's what I do,
I keep trying to be my best,
But on and on goes the pain.
So today,
Today…
I long for God's hand on my shoulder,
Comforting, gently pressed,
Whispering softly as Love's caress:
"Stop now, my sweet child. It's over."

STEPPING OUT

The rain comes out a slate-grey sky.
It monochromes the dappled day,
Brings a sudden change.
Doorways become places of refuge,
Shops havens of dry. Windscreen wipers
Toil frantically, puddles form.
Water pools on awnings,
Waiting for the weight to fall.
It breaks on the pavement below,
Breaking it too.
Inside, the diners order another coffee,
Raise their voices,
Huddle closer to the fire.

And so the rain comes.
This was not forecast.
I step into its tears
Which force me to look at the ground
Where puddles reflect a slate grey sky
And a man with his gaze turned down.

ONCE WE WERE WILD

SWAN

How wild you once were -
To protect your young
A murderer if needs be.
I remember the bloodied mallard floating
Lifelessly in a pond
And you, swan, looming from the water
Your eyes black with violence non-negotiable,
Your wings – a symbol of purity – arched
With the menace of an avalanche
Engulfing all in its path.
Towering, you envelop your foes
In the growing dark of a feathered shroud.
Your intent is terror.
To keep your cygnets safe
You know nothing less
Than to split a resplendent Spring
With savage lightning.

Did the duck die at your hands?
At the strike of the elegant bird

That glides on ponds and lakes,
A fantasy in white of harmony and grace?
Without claws or fangs
Was the blow delivered by the wild power
In the neck's uncoiled embrace?
A mother's fierceness,
An animal white but unchaste?

And then it was your turn.
Death, somehow, came to you.
"I found them on a walk,
Just the wings. Foxes, maybe,
Made off with all the rest,"
And he brought them to his home
In a Bristol suburb.

Now they hang in a garden summerhouse,
By the dartboard, some Turkish weaves,
The tennis rackets and a speaker.
Articulated, they stir something
In us upright animals of blemished flesh,
Puzzling more as memory
Than trophy. Displayed right and left
Like an animate diamond
From a pack of gargantuan cards.
They are so white, it's hard to imagine.

And each feather speaks of ancientness,
Of a world of birdsong alone,
On the ooze of Time, the steady accretions of fertile slime;
Each hollowed bone, each weightless feather,
Each hand turned from claw to delicate fur,
Disturb me, as if a vein of shame shifts subterraneously.
The butchered seraphim tastes suddenly of blood

And sweat and semen in my mouth,
Its shocking fan
Prisms into bruising and battle, sunrise and survival,
And a kind of long lost knowing,
And I hear my yearning calling across ages
With wings, both brute and angel:
"How wild,
How wild, you once were."

THE ANCIENT

The world is an ancient story
That in its telling is far from told.
Too often we walk or talk
Or spin through its mutterings and murmurings, its hum,
As if we are no part of this haiku of unfolding
Driven by the sun.
For this oblivion we stand condemned to fear
The waxing and the waning of light,
As if its gentle ticking were the baying of a mob
From which we must run.
Our feet barely know the ground.
Our heart hammers. We hear its sound
As friendly fire, deadly and bewildering.
Our heads thunder with noise.
The sounds bounce from wall to wall.
We think they must be words,
Searching for sense where there is none.
They are echoes in an echoing chamber,
Far, far, far from the sun.

Yet each day solar flames
Power a story old and new:
We hear its measure in the timpani of breath,
The blood-flood of our pulse.
We sense its step in Spring's renew,
Confounding Winter's seeming death.
And when we sleep, the story goes on,
A mystery unfolding.
Winds kiss the coquettish earth,
Wear her down like a persistent lover,
Now a hurricane of passion, now a spent caress,
Turn her snagging edges to roundness,
Imperceptibly.
Fissures crack and fires spew,
Making fields and lands afresh,
Sprinkling soil from slate-grey ash.
Movements deep, oozing through millenia,
Lower and raise the sea.

And I am here now. A quick intake of breath in the telling
Of a magnificent adventure.
Listen:
A storm makes soft moan,
Loam cracks, limestone sighs,
Buds unravel with quiet yearning,
And sungrown leaves
In a language we have lost but know
Whisper to the wind
Words forever in flow.

DAY

Sometimes the giant, day,
Treads so gently:
As a mother on tiptoed feet
Sprinkles grace
In the sunlit and shadowed places
Of her child's round and restless sleep.

NO HORIZON

Turning, I caught the great arc of day gathering
To a vertigo of grey.
The sun fled from the approaching tide
Like a doe, grazing at ease,
Is of a sudden terrorised
By some dark menace emerging from leaves.
Dorset lanes became all curves,
Nothing kept earth from plunging straight into the sky.
To the eye,
The darkening slate was mauling
The world's very edge,
Beyond the fields, knee deep in clinging clay,
An infinite space, calling.

Reeling, I struggled to my feet.
The wind began buffeting.
Suddenly, without reason,
I tasted all the mistakes I've made,
Felt their weight and grieving.
How many storms would it take

To quiet the fear and loathing?
And how many to come?
I had no way of knowing.

Yet here I was
A little man,
Humbled, helpless, harried,
Pushed by the tilting fury of the sky,
Along with every stinking sod and baffled sheep,
To the world's final faring.
Oaks flail. The sky spins.
Clouds ground. There is no horizon.
Together we hurl into the maelstrom
Though we imagined our roots so deep.
The earth, turning,
Pitches us into her wild embrace, calling,
Dares us to know her,
Falling.

WILD

My wildness is a quiet thing
That cannot bide a name
It is the rise and fall of my chest,
My pulse's beat of back and forth,
Its rhythm of wax and wane.

My wildness is an ancient thing
That echoes through all time
It is the earth teased by eons of wind,
Unfolding, she changes and is the same:
A soil oozing with primeval, fecund slime.

My wildness is in me now,
Latent, not lost.
They tried to tame it
But it would not be denied.
It is one with the music of the spheres
Vibrant in the whorls and vortices of every ear.
I hear it now,

It sings its old old song,
Of how we know one thing,
That we are alive and we belong.

SEVERN ESTUARY

Cresting the field,
I looked towards the horizon,
Mud clinging to expensive boots,
Clods cloying,
Each step weighed
With the effort of yet another day,
And spied there a single tree
And on a branch, a crow,
Perched defiant as a darkling will.
The oak loomed against the sky,
Scratched by a perishing chill.

You talked of Joy Division, positive punk and birding.
Past things and present things. Memories,
The threads that weave,
The stories that tangle us.
We swapped heartfelt tales
But could not hold the other's eye
As we worded the glossy surface of our lives.

I shivered at so many distances.
Or was Dread's cold fingering my soul?

Seeking some kind of cover to Nature I turned,
A pattern that would make sense of it all,
Hedgerow lined with hawthorn,
The gathering of a storm,
Soil fecund and heavy,
Fields of plenty churned.

But that connection was severed generations past.
I looked. An oak hunched.
A corvid cried.
Above the meandering Severn
Winter filled the sky.

INTIMACY

Eyes closed, back erect,
I listen to my breath,
More motion than sound,
Air, the heartbeat of my ground.
Thoughts, though, crowd the space,
And Ego, clothed in thought,
Churns its spumes of froth,
Like a man, drowning, claws the air with cries,
Desperate only to survive:
I plan, therefore I am.
With chatter and intentions it masks the maw of time.

Yet the longing remains to dive deeper into life's stream.
I close my eyes, sit erect,
Try again to be the breather and the breath.
Listening, I hear Physics and Biology tick
In time with Time.
Fleetingly, I touch the resonant void:
In terror, I flee from it.
Beyond the chirping of my mind

A blackbird and a robin sing,
A lawnmower whirrs,
One toe begins to itch.

But I have known Mystery, bathed
In its waters temporal and divine,
Felt it thrill my body
Like a ghost from an ancient land
Guiding spirit home with a golden twine.

I have known a woman run a finger down my spine,
Caress my thigh, with urging entwine
Leg with leg, arm with arm,
And lift us with blood and love
Beyond yours and mine.
And huddled around a hospital bed,
I have heard Mystery tread,
In the silent look, the final sigh
That gifts Farewell from those beyond Goodbye.
And once or twice I have felt Gaia's gentle wings
Gather up my childhood play,
Dusk's birdsong, indigo's wash fast fading away,
And spill contentment on my tongue
Replete with glories bittersweet.
And deep in night's mysterious stream
I have swum in dreams
So achingly true
That, when I wake, though safe at home,
In exile I weep.

For all our clamour, what do we ever know?
Sometimes I think we journey
In a culture unfamiliar yet rich
Hearing only the tongues we have always heard,

Smelling only the scents we have always smelled,
Seeing only the colours we have always seen,
Not knowing that we are and have always been
Sleepers under moon and sun,
Blind, deaf and dumb.

CRY FREEDOM...

MEN

When will we be men,
When, when?
When break the shackles of rage and shame,
Eyes cast down to a ground
In which we find no ground,
Stifling the screams
Of our parched needs
With inaudible apologies
For unspoken dreams?

When will we be men,
When, when,
When look each other in the eye
And know our fierceness
Is not war's blaze,
Or the stifled despair of boys with toys
That rip the hearts of fellow souls,
Rend content
From the homes of others,
Our sisters, our brothers?

When, when?

When,
When will I hold my head high
And in the wind swing my balls,
Spread my arms wide -
So wide the world is but a spark
In the furnace of fathomless space -
And let this flesh and blood
Be seen in all its vulnerability,
Pink, blemished, frail,
Prone to bleed if pricked,
And with pride cry:
"I am a man,
And I take this man to be my brother,
Who stands beside me
Blazing like a sun,
With thin arms and spindle legs,
And ten toes -
Hairy, jointed, stubbed -
Churning between them
In vermiculate coils the clay
From which he is sprung."

When will we be men,
When, when?
When will we know our wound
And let it not reign in our hearts
But gather it in the palm of a hand
As if a fledgling with a broken wing,
A child bird
Fallen from its nest
Calling with terror and yearning
For the safety of home,

A morsel, at least, to eat,
And the enfolding of its mother's breast,
Hot and holding?
When cradle our wound
And love it, as it never was loved
In those far, far away days
When first we took breath
In the stark air of life and death,
And asked for nothing
But gentle moulding?

When bring to our hearts
The kindness we gift
To our own kin?
When, when?

When melt into the embrace
Of a woman's love,
When not run from her fierce grace
And hide in the empty space
Of our boy kings,
Young and old,
Who dwell in the untenented palace
Where their faces alone,
Are reflected in mirrors
Tall, flawless and cold.
When receive her gift
And know in vagina and caress
That her urgent heat
Is the salt, sea and sand of living,
Her beating heart
The tinder, ash and flame of creation
Come to earth
In a body of giving?

When, when?

I stand among men,
And look them in the eye,
Seeing, seen.
In Diptford Hall, we gather,
The sapful tree beneath our feet,
The star-filled night above our heads.
We have journeyed long and far
Helped with strong hand
When each has stumbled on the littered path.
Now we stand aware
That each is whispering to each
Of our wounds and flaws,
And of a touching so elusive,
A touching so in reach.

KINDLY BLOWS

It was a kindly hand that held her arm
And, familiar too, the voice of admonition
That was as wont to carry love as chiding.
In memory, though, it is a jarring,
Some thing of childhood fatefully let slip,
Meant well but landing hard.

She sees that now.
Yet, then, fear supplanted joy
And shame descended like a fog,
Clinging to her hair, her skin,
Seeping into each crease of her limbs,
Finding its way to her stomach.
Her drying mouth tasted of it.
She knew the taste: it is her.

She remembers.

Her mother's eyes sparkling,
Temporary anger spilling through her polished vowels:

"Don't. Don't just go into another's house.
It's naughty. You must ask first. Don't do that again."
And another spark dies.

It was hot and she was SO excited.
Peter had come to play
And they had had such fun in the park,
And there'd been lemonade and ice creams,
And the trampoline.
So when he shrieked and ran she followed
Barely noticing the door, just the sudden cool,
His flailing arms, his thunderous feet.
The first she knew where she was
Was at the sight of faces big and new.
A stranger's house, but with a door
More for in than out
And she meant no ill intent
And life could be so...exquisite.

In memory now, what lingered more,
Was how she must have stared out at her mother
Through those thick, corrective glasses.
Photos showed a puffed up girl
With eyes like toads under the glass.
But it had just been fun. Her mother, though,
Saw something, someone else,
A daughter risking scorn by transgressing a tribal norm.
Mother knew she had had too much of that,
Her bubbly adopted precious girl.
So, with gentle ire, she taught the code
That socialises fire.

Now grown, her house is empty.
Not many thresholds are crossed

Invited or uninvited.
Somehow, it seems, in making her more acceptable to others
She became less acceptable to herself.
She still has the corrective specs
In a box in a box.
She thinks how they helped her see,
Corrected what Nature had carelessly bequeathed.
Yet looking out she wonders if, looking in,
They made monstrous what was plain -
Eyes that welled with longing and tears
Behind a fragile shield of shame.

WORDS

Words are like stones -
The blunt instruments of desire
Poets clash together
On the kitchen table,
Desperate to make fire.

SAILING

When a woman chooses to love
She tarries on the shore.
Carefully, she watches the tides pitch and yaw,
Scanning the enticing blue
For the froth and subdued roar
Of waves breaking on indifferent rocks,
Otherwise hidden from view.
And then, if satisfied,
She submits to the water entirely,
Her body sinking
Into the dangerous depths of two.

When a man chooses to love
He adores the panoramic scene-
The way the hill smoothly slopes, the clifftop juts,
The beach sings and sighs.
Distance beckons,
He is called to try himself,
To master its currents, its storms, its tides.
And then he sails straight out

Until fear -
The impish stowaway -
In roiling waters appears and bids:
"Remember the perils of the deep;
And keep the shoreline near."

DEATH AND OTHER LOCAL DIFFICULTIES

TOO MUCH

Please
Do not make me love you too much
For when the time comes -
And it will be soon -
Whether I reincarnate,
Or rush along a pitch corridor
Into the arms of ecstatic light,
Or simply enrich the loam of some private plot,
I'll miss you,
You, Chinese wisdom, Chinese strength,
You cooking fish,
You moulding a pot,
You in a bathtub, you in a bed,
You at the computer, always playing games,
You laughing, you crying, you caring,
You enjoying, you in shame,
You, smell, you, touch, you, song.
Please.
Please.

Like the stars suddenly gone.

HUNGER

When they entered she was scared,
And cowered under a rain of boots and barking voices.
Their rough ways, their youth long gone,
They were like those who separated her
From mother and father,
Never to see them again.

She had got used to that -
The habit of being alone
Even when they – the orphans – packed
Bullets into boxes with exhausted fingers, fought
For threadbare blankets, huddled
For warmth seven to a bunk
In that frigid camp.
Survive. Alone. Yes, she thought, I'm used to that.

But the hunger – the great gaping yearning
That lived even in her dreams
And made hands claws
When the guards distributed the gruel,

The scraps that fuelled only keener yearning,
Until the next mocking meal.
She never got used to that.

Strange then that the bread she snatched
From his dirty Russian fingers
Should satisfy her less
Than the kindly arm he wrapped around her shoulders
In a hug tenderly unrestrained,
Which breached the watchtowers of a heart,
Bringing daddy and mummy back,
Only to steal them away again.

THE BOX

I found the box beneath a pile of handbags.
A faint smell of leather scented the stifled air
Which at last could breathe again
After all the years of waiting.
The label, though old, was clear:
A Kodak Eastman projector 2000.
How long it had lain unused
I did not know -
Thirty, even forty years, maybe,
When the house rang to the sound of young lives
Imperceptibly deviating off line.
The square box had stayed in its place
With the patience of a craftsman
Who knows how to make something well
Whatever bedlam less quiet folk create.
I felt the magic lamp, eager
To release its genie.
It was heavy with industry and precision
As I lifted it clear.
It appeared ready again to make memories.

I show the find to my mother and suggest
We have a slide show.
I know no other way for us to just be.
And I remember that on other long- ago picture nights
Comforting wings seemed to enfold our hurting brood.
Surely this squat mechanical hen could lay her eggs
To such rich effect once again.

I plug in the machine
And it works of course.
Electricity sparks it into life;
Bulb, glass, copper and circuit combine.
The fan, which cools the engine, whirs
Through the echoing spaces
Mother and I go as we watch familial ghosts
Flicker in the focused light.
Goodnaturedly, we argue over dates and places,
The usual sort of thing,
Wonder at those flared trousers, that haircut,
How often that Ford broke down,
The things we had shared, the sights we had seen,
Before settling into silence
Over people and faces dead
As a ring is -
Gold yet cold on the projected screen.
But our deepest sadness, I suspect,
Is reserved for the living,
Who carry so carelessly so many tender things.

Soon our reverie is disturbed, the show cannot go on.
A black shadow is now obscuring each slide.
Quickly we slip into distance and frustration.

So I pack the box away, uncomfortable

With memories and Kodachrome feelings.
The projector's fan is silent, its intense light fallen dark.
I admire its craft.
It is well made, knowing then and now
Its form and function.
A new part should readily that shadow mend,
But, for the boxed things of our lives, I sense
There is no painless healing.

NOISES OFF

Embraced by a restless solitude
I hear noises off. It hits like an awakening.
There is a crowd of children cheering
Some team of football players, to me, unseen.
I imagine the young boys and girls
Doing as I used to do,
Chasing the ball like a magnet
On a ridiculously sloping pitch,
Their fresh legs goose-pimpled,
Their shirts covered with mud and sweat,
Their shorts stained with green.

The voices of the young crowd carry
In the air,
Like birdsong
But distinctly human in their aim
To have their side win.
Yet there is something, too,
In their unbroken cries,
Which celebrates the playing and the game.

Listening, I feel the sound and the silence
Wrap around me their arms of stillness,
Whispering with slackening comfort in my ear:
"There is life, vibrant and innocent,
And we're here,
We're here, we're here."

It is so unlike that other awakening,
When stirring from an unbidden afternoon sleep
Into a too real silence mixed,
In terror at my little death, I grieve for
How much life I just have
And how much, how much,
When I die, I will
Forever miss.

ENDING ON A HIGH NOTE... JOY AND OTHER CELEBRATIONS

HEROES

Caught off guard by a swelling chord,
The shrieks of joy, the jubilation, the applause
"He's done it," slips through
Where direct acclaim has failed to do.
It pierces something guarded,
The shield where faults dare not yield.
I watch as he sinks to his knees,
Lifted, at last, of the expectation
Weighted year after year;
They slide down his cheeks,
Surrendering finally to self compassion,
Forgiven, released, the tears.
Crossing the line at triumph's moment, his peak,
He becomes of a sudden a grown man no longer
But a boy with no place he must reach.
He breaks with relief:
At last he is all right.
Then I too shed tears at the finish,
Let slip grieving acclaim
For us, the heroes without applause,

Who everyday line up in our lanes
And keep going despite knowing
There will be no moment of summation,
No recognition for each morning drawing back the covers
To plant one foot after another
On a cold pine floor.
Each one of us an unsung hero,
Always falling short,
Our arcs never complete,
Yet stubbornly, courageously,
Facing mortality's silent white line.
Music does not background our action,
Narrative not shape our day,
But again and again we bay,
"I do not know if I am enough, or will ever be,
But when a brother attains a haven, I rejoice,
Though I face a fathomless sea."

SANTIAGO DE COMPOSTELA

Blown South by a storm
I journeyed to Santiago de Compostela.
I had longed to be renewed in my chosen way,
By the sun's caress, the sea's spittle and spray,
Its salt abrasive on the skin. Its winds, bracing.
But in Ferrol I found the town dead
And rain forecast for the following day.
So I converted to pilgrim, by train caminhoed to Santiago,
"There, if it rains, at least in the Cathedral I can stay."

So it was I found this great church,
This cloister of icons and animate beings.
There, teenage girls in groups had keener looks
For a boy, awkward yet burgeoning,
Than The Virgin Mary's lifeless gaze,
Or yet another martyr's mangled hands and gold-leafed hood.
My heart yearned to know: "Is God really in this place?"
Columns of Purbeck marble disappeared in a dismal nave,
Gaudy trumpets blazed in silence around His plastic face.
Priests sat to hear confessions, one euro at a time.

Christ's blood dripped. It flowed in crimson.

Despairing I followed the sign to "el tresor"
Hoping that a craftsman's skill might stir my faith.
And there, along the way, hidden in that shrine's depths,
I found tapestries with no heaven or hell in sight.
The weavers had made a world I knew -
A Medieval party oiled by lust and booze.
Tinkers and maidens dance in joy
Men lech – and women too -
A landlady ejects a troublemaker with a broom,
Ploughmen drink and squabble over dice,
But most wonderful of all,
In that place of reverence and brazen piety,
Depicted in thread, a man, who's had too many,
Has his cock out and pisses on a wall.

Thank God for human beings,
The makers of lust and love,
The brewers of sack and pee, the crafters of clay and mud.
Thank God for the weavers of cotton,
Observing life in a stitch,
The living of it, the wasting of it;
Revering the colours of the sky,
Revelling in the music of the ditch.

Is this the question that draws the pilgrims here,
"Who should I thank or curse for all this?"
Is that why on Easter Day it's
Human hands that blister to make bells ring,
Men, women and children of surging blood
That shape breath to verse in exultation:
It's people, people, who sing.

My conversion is complete.
I return to the salt of the sea,
And to a woman's hot arms held out to me.
I take a leak and recall
The Cathedral's crypted mess.
Could Heaven be anything more?
Is life anything less?

RUHEVOLL

The swell of cellos and violins
Release soft rain on weary limbs,
Each drawn bow a drop
Falling from calm sky,
Each note an anointing tear of love,
As if my daughter was hanging happily on my heavy legs,
My lover's moan running cool along the thigh,
A cloud's dappled shadow a soothing
In the rivers of the ribs.
Each returning bow, hovering on the strings,
Cascades with yearning the feet that carry,
The hands that touch the world,
Making them as new as lovers are
When together's first awakening shows
Dawn for what it is -
The immanence of flowering
In sunlight's bud, like a kiss,
Yet unfurled.
A falling cadence caresses now my lips,
Expectation of its resolution

A kind of memory for my aching back
Of the cycles of the land.
Breathing, I resonate to a basoon's steady breath,
Recognise its strength is that of a father's hand.

I can lie naked here,
Every kind word and act,
Through sting and life's indifferent blows,
Drenching down in arching phrase.
I could die, ruhevoll,
Baptised in music's blessings,
By passion's quavers rinsed,
Exultant in joy raining from above.
But now the day is mine to live,
And ground and sky and love.

ACKNOWLEDGMENTS

Thanks to everyone who has inspired me and encouraged me along the way. You know who you are. Especial thanks to my family and Tony, Billy, Neil, Anna and Penny, who helped me through the dark days and Jen and her boys, Corben and Joshua, who have lighted my way through the brighter ones.

Thanks also to Charlotte and Adam Nicholls who gave their time to guide me through this process. They have been so generous.

Finally, thanks to every tree that spreads, every bird that sings, every wind that blows and every soil that sweats...my ground, my inspiration.

ABOUT THE AUTHOR

David Glasman was born in the border country between Muswell Hill and Wood Green in London. He started his working life as a journalist before re-training as a psychologist, after spending almost a year in South America. On moving to Frome, Somerset, he found he had a lifetime of writing, which he then set about editing. This book is the first fruit of that labour.

You can contact Davis Glasman at:
david.glasman@yahoo.co.uk

Printed in Great Britain
by Amazon